Written to give us hope

'Everything that was written long ago was written for our instruction. Its aim was to enable us, through the fortitude and encouragement which the Scriptures give, to maintain our hope'
Romans 15:4, *The New Testament: A Translation by William Barclay* (Arthur James).

The Christian hope has seen everything and endured everything, but it has not despaired. It is not hope in human goodness or human achievement. It is hope in the power of God. Our hope is maintained by exposure to God's revelation in Scripture. We maintain it *'While we wait for the blessed hope – the glorious appearing of our great God and Saviour, Jesus Christ'*
Titus 2:13.

Hope is
a shining light

Hope, like the gleaming taper's light,
Adorns and cheers our way;
And still, as darker grows the night,
Emits a brighter ray.
Oliver Goldsmith

In the darkness of this world, when
troubles often eclipse the sun, hope
is a light reminding us that better
times are on the way.

Hope is a dream

Hope is the dream
of a waking man.
Pliny the Elder

It's the dream that will not
vanish into vapour with the
coming of the Morning.
Stay awake and keep your
dreams of hope alive.

Hope is vital!

Hope is necessary in every condition.

Samuel Johnson

We can't live without hope. Whoever you are, whatever your circumstances, you need to have hope for a bright tomorrow.

Hope is a gift
from God

No man is able of himself to grasp the supreme good of eternal life; he needs divine help. Hence there is here a two-fold object, the eternal life we hope for; and the divine help we hope by.
Thomas Aquinas

God gives us the promise of eternal life, and then gives us the hope we need to cling to that promise. Accept and cling to the proffered gift.

Hope keeps the engine turning

Hope is one of the principal springs that keep mankind in motion.

Andrew Fuller

If you don't wish to come to a grinding halt, hang on to hope.

Hope is like a bird?

Hope is the thing with feathers
That perches in the soul.
And sings the tune
Without the words,
And never stops at all.
Emily Dickinson

As the birds sing in the depths of winter, certain of the coming spring, so hope 'sings' in the soul, even when the days are dark and cold.

It's as necessary as the air we breathe

What oxygen is to the lungs, such is hope for the meaning of life.
Emil Brunner

Make sure you stay connected to the Source of hope to keep the oxygen flowing!

Hope isn't always the easiest option

Hope is putting faith to work when doubting would be easier.

Anon

Hope accentuates the positive and eliminates the negative.

A sure and certain hope

Hope is the unshakeable certainty in the realisation of the promises of God in Jesus Christ, based on Jesus' life, death and resurrection.
Tissa Balasuriya

Hold on! Don't waver! God's promises are certain and sure. Your hopes *will* be realised.

Faith and hope go hand in hand

*Hope is faith holding
out its hand in the dark.*
George Iles

When we stretch out our
hand to him, his hand will
hold ours fast (Psalm 139:10)
and never let go.

Faith and hope – you can't have one without the other!

Hope is hearing the melody of the future. Faith is to dance it.
Rubem Alves

Keep your ears open and your feet in step!

Faith, hope . . . and love – three things that will last forever

Faith goes up the stairs that love has made and looks out of the windows which hope has opened.
Charles Spurgeon

Make sure you don't close the windows!

Have confidence!

Faith is the confidence that what we hope for will actually happen.
Hebrews 11:1, NLT

What you hope for *will* come true!

Faith and hope are two sides of the same coin

The word 'hope' I take for faith; and indeed hope is nothing else but the constancy of faith.
John Calvin

Keep plenty of this currency in your spiritual bank account.

The secret of true beauty?

*Hope is beautiful, and
so are those who have it.*
Cathy Rowland

A hopeful person is beautiful
on the inside and the outside.

A healing balm for sorrow

Hope is the physician
of each misery.
Irish proverb

Hope fixes your eyes on the
unseen and so the things
which are seen are in less
sharp focus.

God, our hope

O Lord, you alone are my hope.
I've trusted you, O Lord, from
childhood. . . . I will keep on
hoping for your help; I will praise
you more and more.
Psalm 71:5, 14, NLT

Place your hope in the only One
who can be trusted not to fail you.

Make sure your hopes are built on the right foundation – Jesus Christ

My hope is built on nothing less
Than Jesus' blood and
righteousness. . . .
On Christ the solid rock I stand,
All other ground is sinking sand.
Edward Mote

Hopes placed on anything or anyone else are doomed to failure.

Hope to be found in the Word

I wait for the LORD, my soul waits, and in his word I put my hope. . . . O Israel, put your hope in the LORD, for with the LORD is unfailing love and with him is full redemption.
Psalm 130:5, 7

God's Word reveals a bright future in store.

Life getting you down?

Remember your word to your servant, for you have given me hope. . . . My soul faints with longing for your salvation, . . . You are my refuge and my shield; I have put my hope in your word.
Psalm 119:49, 81, 114

Find comfort and hope in the Word.

When you're in the darkest
tunnel or the deepest pit . . .

*I waited patiently for the LORD; he
turned to me and heard my cry. He
lifted me out of the slimy pit, out of
the mud and mire; he set my feet on
a rock and gave me a firm place to
stand.*
Psalm 40: 1, 2

Keep waiting and hoping.
Rescue is just around the
corner.

Feeling
depressed?

Why are you downcast, O my soul?
Why so disturbed within me? Put
your hope in God, for I will yet praise
him, my Saviour and my God.
Psalm 42:5

Hope is your exit ticket
from the Slough of Despond.

Why worry when you can hope?

Be strong and courageous. Do not be afraid or terrified . . . , for the LORD your God goes with you; he will never leave you nor forsake you.
Deuteronomy 31:6

You're not in this alone.

Words written with *you* in mind

For everything that was written in the past was written to teach us, so that through endurance and the encouragement of the Scriptures we might have hope.
Romans 15:4

Keep reading to feed your hope.

The Lord, our hope

The LORD also shall roar out of Zion, and utter his voice from Jerusalem; and the heavens and the earth shall shake: but the LORD will be the hope of his people, and the strength of the children of Israel.
Joel 3:16, KJV

He's your only hope and strength in the day of trouble.

A fail-safe assurance

O God our help in ages past.
Our hope for years to come.
Isaac Watts

However bad life gets,
remember God's leading
in the past and be assured
of his guidance and protection
for the future. He'll never let
you down.

Don't despair

It is not hard for the Lord to turn night into day. He that sends the clouds can as easily clear the skies. Let us be of good cheer. It is better farther on. Let us sing Hallelujah by anticipation.
Charles Spurgeon

Things *will* get better, so start singing!

The God of hope has a listening ear

For in You, O LORD, I hope; You will hear, O Lord my God.
Psalm 38:15, NKJV

Make sure you share your hopes and dreams with him.

The God of hope is also the source of joy and peace

Oh! May the God of green hope fill you up with joy, fill you up with peace, so that your believing lives, filled with the life-giving energy of the Holy Spirit, will brim over with hope!
Romans 15:13, MGE

Is *your* cup of hope brimming over?

Jesus is our hope
(1 Tim 1:1)

Precious Name, O how sweet!
Hope of earth and joy of
Heav'n.
Lydia O. Baxter

If you want the joy, keep
connected to the Source
of hope.

When you think you're sinking . . .

His oath, His covenant, His blood,
Support me in the whelming flood.
When all around my soul gives way,
He then is all my Hope and Stay.
Edward Mote

When you're drowning in a sea of troubles, hope is an anchor that prevents shipwreck.

The God of hope gives peace in the storm

To all who are tossed by the waves,
you are the calm of the harbour;
you are the hope of the hopeful.
Severus of Thrace (martyred c. 304)

Steer your storm-tossed ship's course towards Hope Harbour.

A source of happiness

But blessed are those who trust in the Lord and have made the Lord their hope and confidence.
Jeremiah 17:7, NLT

If you want to be happy, be hopeful.

Dr Hope?

Hope, the patent medicine
For disease, disaster, sin.
Wallace Rice

Hope is God's cure-all for
the problems in this life.

A preventative medicine?

*If it were not for hope,
the heart would break.*
Thomas Fuller

Wholehearted hope keeps
you whole-hearted.

Hope is the
best medicine

*There is no medicine like hope,
no incentive so great, and no tonic
so powerful as expectations of
something tomorrow.*
Orison Swett Marden

Don't neglect to take generous
doses of this God-given elixir.

If you want to stay well, keep your hopes alive

If you lose hope, somehow you lose the vitality that keeps life moving, you lose that courage to be, that quality that helps you go on in spite of it all.
Martin Luther King Jr

Lack of hope will have a devastating effect on your health and well-being.

The final cure for heartsickness is hope fulfilled

Hope deferred makes the heart sick,
but a longing fulfilled is a tree of life.
Proverbs 13:12

Keep hoping, as the fulfilment
of your hopes is just around
the corner.

A cause for rejoicing?

Hope fills the afflicted soul with such inward joy and consolation, that it can laugh while tears are in the eye, sigh and sing all in a breath; it is called 'the rejoicing of hope' (Hebrews 3:6).
William Gurnall

Yes, even in the darkest of situations we can be happy because of the hope we have.

A reason to be happy

Be joyful in hope, . . .
Romans 12:12

The hopeful Christian has no excuse for being miserable.

Hope = happiness

*Hope is itself a species of happiness,
and perhaps, the chief happiness
which the world affords.*
Samuel Johnson

So smile, because there are
wonderful things in store
for you.

Cultivate the habit of hoping

Practise hope. As hopefulness becomes a habit, you can achieve a permanently happy spirit.
Norman Vincent Peale

Practice makes perfect! The habit of hoping will make you joyful.

Rejoice in sufferings?

A religious hope does not only bear up the mind under her sufferings, but makes her rejoice in them.
Joseph Addison

Yes, because with hope you can see through them to the ultimate goal.

Rejoice in hope

And we rejoice in the hope of the glory of God. Not only so, but we also rejoice in our sufferings, because we know that suffering produces perseverance; perseverance, character; and character, hope. And hope does not disappoint us, because God has poured out his love into our hearts by the Holy Spirit, whom he has given us.
Romans 5:2-5

Ours is the hope that won't disappoint.

Cultivate a positive attitude

We are all in the gutter,
but some of us are looking
at the stars.
Oscar Wilde

Are *your* eyes fixed
heavenward?

Hope is an encourager

When the world says, 'Give up,' Hope whispers, 'Try it one more time.'

Anon

Are you listening to that whisper?

Whispering hope

Soft as the voice of an angel,
Breathing a lesson unheard,
Hope with a gentle persuasion
Whispers her comforting word:
Wait till the darkness is over,
Wait till the tempest is done,
Hope for the sunshine tomorrow,
After the shower is gone.
Septimus Winner

In the midst of the downpour, Hope whispers, 'The sun will come out tomorrow.'

Hoping
against hope

Against all hope, Abraham in hope believed and so became the father of many nations, just as it had been said to him, 'So shall your offspring be.'
Romans 4:18

Take a leaf out of Abraham's book. Keep hoping, even when the situation appears hopeless.

Remember: *nothing* is impossible with God (Luke 1:37)

There are no hopeless situations, only people who think hopelessly.
Windred Newman

The word *impossible* isn't in God's vocabulary.

Never give up hope!

Never let your head hang down.
Never give up and sit down and
grieve. Find another way. And don't
pray when it rains if you don't pray
when the sun shines.
Satchel Paige

It's always too early to
abandon hope (Mary Manin
Morrissey), so keep hoping!

Don't put yourself on a starvation diet!

To eat bread without hope is still slowly to starve to death.
Pearl S. Buck

Make sure your spiritual diet has generous helpings of hope.

When the chips are down, still keep hoping . . .

We must accept finite disappointment,
but we must never lose infinite hope.
Martin Luther King Jr

The hope God gives us
is limitless.

In the absence of hope, what happens?

When hope is taken away from a people, moral degeneration follows swiftly thereafter.
Pearl S. Buck

If hope were not, heart would break.
(13th century proverb)

Hope is vital for emotional and spiritual well-being.

Godlessness = hopelessness

... remember that at that time you were separate from Christ, excluded from citizenship in Israel and foreigners to the covenants of the promise, without hope and without God in the world.
Ephesians 2:12

No Christ, no hope.

Hope assures us of a faithful companion

We have come to share in Christ if we hold firmly till the end the confidence we had at first.
Hebrews 3:14

Make sure your hope doesn't waver!

You have two choices

The hope of the righteous shall be gladness: but the expectation of the wicked shall perish.
Proverbs 10:28, KJV

Hopelessness is a very bleak option.

How would we cope without hope?

Ah, Hope! what would life be,
stripped of thy encouraging smiles,
that teach us to look behind the dark
clouds of today, for the golden beams
that are to gild the morrow.
Susanna Moodie

Hope gives us strength for
today as well as the promise
of a bright future.

To hope or not to hope?

If you do not hope, you will not find what is beyond your hopes.
Clement of Alexandria

Give up hope and your hope will never be realised.

Hopeless end or endless hope?

Other men see only a hopeless end, but the Christian rejoices in an endless hope.

Gilbert M. Beeken

Be wise and choose the preferable philosophy.

Hope is essential

No vision and you perish;
No Ideal, and you're lost;
Your heart must ever cherish
Some faith at any cost.
Some hope, some dream to cling to,
Some rainbow in the sky,
Some melody to sing to,
Some service that is high.
Harriet Du Autermont

Without hope, doom and
gloom are the only options.

Without hope, what's the point?

Life without hope is an empty, boring, and useless life. I cannot imagine that I could strive for something if I did not carry hope in me. I am thankful to God for this gift. It is as big as life itself.
Vaclav Havel

Life is a gift and hope is the gift that makes life worthwhile.

You've got to have hope

Without hope life is meaningless. Without hope life is meaning less and less.

Anon

Hope gives your life direction and purpose.

You're well fed. But remember, others are hungry.

People are hungry for messages of hope and life.
Morgan Brittany

Share your hope with the hope-starved.

Question: Where would
we be without hope?

*Without Christ there is
no hope.*
Charles Spurgeon

Answer: HOPELESS!

Without hope, there's no incentive to try

Where there is no hope, there can be no endeavour.
Samuel Johnson

Keep hoping and keep doing your best in all the tasks before you.

Those who hope in the Lord are promised strength

Be of good courage, And he shall strengthen your heart, All you who hope in the LORD.
Psalm 31:24, NKJV

God will provide the strength you need to face life's battles, as long as your hopes are centred in him.

God has
a plan for you

*And we know that God causes
everything to work together for
the good of those who love God
and are called according to his
purpose for them.*
Romans 8:28, NLT

God is the master architect
of your life and he has firm
hold of the blueprints.

Remember!

Yet this I call to mind and therefore I have hope: Because of the LORD's great love we are not consumed, for his compassions never fail. They are new every morning; great is your faithfulness.
Lamentations 3:21-23

Don't forget God's faithfulness.

Cheer up. Troubles won't last forever.

For our present troubles are small and won't last very long. Yet they produce for us a glory that vastly outweighs them and will last forever!
2 Corinthians 4:17, NLT

Hope sees through troubles to the never-ending glory to come.

Hope confidently!

Hold your head high, stick your chest out. You can make it. It gets dark sometimes, but morning comes. . . . Keep hope alive.
Jesse Jackson

Hope catches the glimmer of light at the end of the tunnel.

Feeling defeated?

Here on earth you will have many trials and sorrows. But take heart, because I have overcome the world.
John 16:33, NLT

Hope will make *you* an overcomer, too.

Be a messenger of hope

Those who keep speaking about the sun while walking under a cloudy sky are messengers of hope, the true saints of our day.
Henri J. Nouwen

What's *your* weather forecast?

When the worst comes to the worst, still keep hoping

Even though I walk through the valley of the shadow of death, I will fear no evil, for you are with me; your rod and your staff, they comfort me.
Psalm 23:4

You have a constant companion who'll see you through.

Even when everything seems hopeless, be assured that things will get better one day

Sometimes our fate resembles a fruit tree in winter. Who would think that those branches would turn green again and blossom, but we hope it, we know it.
Johann Wolfgang von Goethe

It may be winter now but spring is on the way!

In the dark times, cling on to hope

Joy in affliction is rooted in the hope of resurrection, but our experience of suffering also deepens the root of that hope.
John Piper

As in periods of drought a tree's roots dig deeper into the soil for sustenance, so in times of suffering hope digs deeper roots and finds water for the thirsty soul.

In painful and stressful times . . .

Through trials deep and conflicts sore,
Yet still a smile of joy he wore;
I asked what buoyed his spirits up,
'O this!' said he – 'the blessèd hope.'
Annie R. Smith

. . . hope will put a smile on your face.

You have a bright future ahead of you

'For I know the plans I have for you,' says the Lord. 'They are plans for good and not for disaster, to give you a future and a hope.'
Jeremiah 29:11, NLT

Our generous God has wonderful plans in store, so hope and trust.

Hope is
an anchor

*We have run to God for safety.
Now his promises should greatly
encourage us to take hold of the
hope that is right in front of us.
This hope is like a firm and
steady anchor for our souls.*
Hebrews 6:18, 19, CEV

Will your anchor hold in
the storm?

Where is your hope centred?

Don't put your confidence in powerful people; there is no help for you there. . . . But joyful are those who have the God of Israel as their helper, whose hope is in the Lord their God.
Psalm 146:3, 5, NLT

There's only One you can trust to fulfil your hopes.

Hope for the diligent seeker

If you look for me wholeheartedly, you will find me.
Jeremiah 29:13, NLT

Half-hearted hope will not win the prize.

When you find him and he dwells in you . . .

. . . Christ in you, the hope of glory.
Colossians 1:27

. . . the brightest future you can imagine is assured.

Hope of victory

But thanks be to God! He gives us the victory through our Lord Jesus Christ.
1 Cor. 15:57

You can be a conqueror if you keep hoping!

Hope to conquer all obstacles

I can do everything through him who gives me strength.
Philippians 4:13

No more defeatism! You *can* get through with him by your side!

Saving hope

And this hope is what saves us. But if we already have what we hope for, there is no need to keep on hoping. However, we hope for something we have not yet seen, and we patiently wait for it.
Romans 8:24, 25, CEV

Keep hoping and be patient – your salvation depends on it.

Dietary advice?

Suggestions for fasting and feasting: fast from discontent; feast on thankfulness. Fast from worry; feast on trust. . . . Fast from unrelenting pressures; feast on unceasing prayers. . . . Fast from discouragement, **feast on hope.**
Anon

Do you make hope part of your daily spiritual diet?

Hope is God's gift to a hopeless world

The word which God has written on the brow of every man is Hope.
Victor Hugo

This gift is offered to *you*, so accept it!

Prisoners of hope?

There is no better or more blessed bondage than to be a prisoner of hope.

Roy Z. Kemp

Hope holds us captive because it promises wonderful freedom to come.

Hope for a sick world

On the earth, nations will be in anguish and perplexity at the roaring and tossing of the sea. Men will faint from terror, apprehensive of what is coming on the world, . . . At that time they will see the Son of Man coming in a cloud with power and great glory. Luke 21:25-27

Yes, things are getting bad, but look up, because the Rescuer is on the way!

Heavenly armour

But since we belong to the day, let us be self-controlled, putting on faith and love as a breastplate, and the hope of salvation as a helmet.
1 Thessalonians 5:8

Are you properly dressed?

We're getting nearer

. . . one far-off divine event,
To which the whole creation
moves.
Alfred, Lord Tennyson

We're all heading inexorably
towards the moment of God's
final intervention.

Never doubt it!

Jesus has been taken from you into heaven, but someday he will return from heaven in the same way you saw him go!
Acts 1:11, NLT

He promised he'd come back and he always keeps his promises.

It's the
blessed hope

*Looking for that blessed hope, and
the glorious appearing of the great
God and our Saviour Jesus Christ;*
Titus 2:13, KJV

Keep your eyes peeled,
because he's coming!

Feeling fearful?

*Energise the limp hands, strengthen
the rubbery knees. Tell fearful souls,
'Courage! Take heart! God is here,
right here, on his way to put things
right and redress all wrongs. He's
on his way! He'll save you!'*
Isaiah 35:3, 4, MGE

Take courage! He's coming
to save you.

There'll be no mistaking that event

For as lightning that comes from the east is visible even in the west, so will be the coming of the Son of Man.
Matthew 24:27

Make sure you're ready for it!

The waiting is over

And it shall be said in that day, Lo, this is our God; we have waited for him, and he will save us: this is the LORD; we have waited for him, we will be glad and rejoice in his salvation.
Isaiah 25:9, KJV

The final consummation of our hope will be a day of wonderful rejoicing.

It's resurrection morning!

For the Lord himself will come down from heaven, with a loud command, with the voice of the archangel and with the trumpet call of God, and the dead in Christ will rise first. After that, we who are still alive and are left will be caught up together with them in the clouds to meet the Lord in the air.
1 Thessalonians 4:16, 17

When that day comes we'll be walking on air!

A glorious promise!

Dear friends, now we are children of God, and what we will be has not yet been made known. But we know that when he appears, we shall be like him, for we shall see him as he is.
1 John 3:2

We can only see dimly at the moment, but on that day we'll see him face to face.

Eyesight problems?

We don't yet see things clearly. We're squinting in a fog, peering through a mist. But it won't be long before the weather clears and the sun shines bright! We'll see it all then, see it all as clearly as God sees us, knowing him directly just as he knows us!
1 Corinthians 13:12, MGE

20/20 vision is promised on that day.

An incredible metamorphosis!

And we eagerly await a Saviour from . . . [heaven], the Lord Jesus Christ, who . . . will transform our lowly bodies so that they will be like his glorious body.
Philippians 3:20-21

From caterpillar to butterfly!

A cast-iron guarantee!

Jesus said . . . , 'I am the resurrection and the life. He who believes in me will live, even though he dies.'
John 11:25

Jesus' resurrection is living proof that yours is to come if you hang on to hope!

A crown awaits you!

And when the Great Shepherd appears, you will receive a crown of never-ending glory and honour.
1 Peter 5:4, NLT

God's going to share his Kingdom with *you!*

The hope
of reunion

*For since we believe that
Jesus died and was raised
to life again, we also believe
that when Jesus returns, God
will bring back with him the
believers who have died.*
1 Thessalonians 4:14, NLT

Reunited, never more to part!

Our forever Friend

And so we will be with the Lord forever.
1 Thessalonians 4:17

We'll also be united with the One who has made it all possible.

Instant and complete transformation

Listen, I tell you a mystery: We will not all sleep, but we will all be changed – in a flash, in the twinkling of an eye, at the last trumpet. For the trumpet will sound, the dead will be raised imperishable, and we will be changed. For the perishable must clothe itself with the imperishable, and the mortal with immortality.
1 Corinthians 15:51-53

The hope of immortality will be realised.

A great change is coming

If a man dies, will he live again?
All the days of my hard service I
will wait for my renewal to come.
You will call and I will answer you;
you will long for the creature your
hands have made.
Job 14:14, 15

Be ready to answer that call.

You'd better believe it!

In hope of eternal life, which God, that cannot lie, promised before the world began.
Titus 1:2, KJV

The Lamb slain from the foundation of the world is coming to take you home.

Victory over death

Everyone who lives in me and believes in me will never ever die.
John 11:26, NLT

So believe and hope and share in that victory!

Death, **thou** shalt die!
(John Donne)

Then, when our dying bodies have been transformed into bodies that will never die, this Scripture will be fulfilled: 'Death is swallowed up in victory. O death, where is your victory? O death, where is your sting?'
1 Corinthians 15:54, 55, NLT

The last enemy will be conquered, so you have nothing to fear.

There'll be no dark valley when Jesus comes

And God shall wipe away all tears from their eyes; and there shall be no more death, neither sorrow, nor crying, neither shall there be any more pain: for the former things are passed away.
Revelation 21:4, KJV

That day heralds the end to suffering and sin.

All my trials, Lord, soon be over

Pain cannot exist in the atmosphere of heaven. There will be no more tears, no funeral trains, no badges of mourning. . . . 'The inhabitant shall not say, I am sick: the people that dwell therein shall be forgiven their iniquity.' Isaiah 33:24.
Ellen G. White

The end of the Great Controversy signals joy forevermore!

No remembrance of things past

You will surely forget your trouble, recalling it only as waters gone by. Life will be brighter than noonday, and darkness will become like morning. You will be secure, because there is hope; you will look about you and take your rest in safety.
Job 11:16-18

All the bad things are forgotten as a dream turns to vapour in the morning light.

Heavenly music?

O sweet, celestial music,
Heard from a land afar –
The song of Heav'n and Homeland,
Thro' doors God leaves ajar!
E. E. Rexford

Hope helps you to catch
a sound of the singing.

Beyond your wildest imaginings

And yet, 'eye hath not seen, nor ear heard, neither have entered into the heart of man, the things which God hath prepared for them that love Him.' 1 Corinthians 2:9. Human language is inadequate to describe the reward of the righteous. It will be known only to those who behold it. No finite mind can comprehend the glory of the Paradise of God.
Ellen G. White

It may be unimaginably wonderful, but believe it, because it's coming!

Great expectations

Praise be to the God and Father of our Lord Jesus Christ! In his great mercy he has given us new birth into a living hope through the resurrection of Jesus Christ from the dead, and into an inheritance that can never perish, spoil or fade – kept in heaven for you.'
1 Peter 1:3, 4

There's a rich inheritance in store for you.

Never-ending pleasure!

*You have made known to me
the path of life; you will fill
me with joy in your presence,
with eternal pleasures at
your right hand.*
Psalm 16:11

Walk beside him here and
you'll be at his side then.

A marvellous future lies ahead

The future is as bright as the promises of God.

Adoniram Judson

His wonderful promises won't disappoint.

There's a 'des res' for you

In my Father's house are many rooms; . . . I am going there to prepare a place for you . . . that you also may be where I am.
John 14:2-4

And you'll have the best neighbour in the world!

The ultimate
divine makeover

*Then I saw a new heaven and a new
earth, for the old heaven and the old
earth had disappeared. . . . And the
one sitting on the throne said, 'Look,
I am making everything new!'*
Revelation 21:1, 5, NLT

New Heaven, new Earth,
brand new you!

God will be with us in person

I heard a loud shout from the throne, saying, 'Look, God's home is now among his people! He will live with them, and they will be his people. God himself will be with them.'
Revelation 21:3, NLT

If he's been your close companion here, he'll be even closer there.

Want to be wise?

All human wisdom is summed up in two words – wait and hope.
Alexander Dumas

The LORD is good to those whose hope is in him, to the one who seeks him; it is good to wait quietly for the salvation of the LORD.
Lamentations 3:25, 26

Hold on! It's coming!

Though it tarries, wait for it

The longest day must have its close –
the gloomiest night will wear on to a
morning. An eternal, inexorable lapse
of moments is ever hurrying the day
of the evil to an eternal night, and the
night of the just to an eternal day.
Harriet Beecher Stowe

The day is coming and the
best is yet to be! Believe it!

Don't throw in the towel

So do not throw away your confidence; it will be richly rewarded. You need to persevere so that when you have done the will of God, you will receive what he has promised. For in just a very little while, 'He who is coming will come and will not delay.' Hebrews 10:35-37

Stay faithful and your perseverance will be rewarded.

His coming is getting nearer!

Behold, I am coming soon!
My reward is with me,
and I will give to everyone
according to what he
has done.
Revelation 22:12

And he's not coming
empty-handed!

Read the signs of the times!

So when all these things begin to happen, stand and look up, for your salvation is near!
Luke 21:28, NLT

Stand tall! Head up! Be ready!

Hold on just a little longer . . .

'Yes, I am coming soon.'
Amen. Come, Lord Jesus.
Revelation 22:20

He's almost here!